THE KITCHEN LIBRARY

PRESERVES & PICKLES

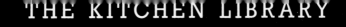

THE KITCHEN LIBRARY

PRESERVES
& PICKLES

Heather Lambert

OCTOPUS BOOKS

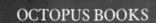

Harmon
Jam.

Mixed Fruit
Marmalade

pple Jelly
Boxquer gam

Strawberry
Conserve.

Grape
Conserve.

Scottish
Curd

Banana
Chutney.

Cranberry
Relish.

Cucumber and

Apple and Raspberry
Cheese

Cucumber &
Cherry
Chutney.

CONTENTS

This edition published 1989 by
Octopus Books Limited
a division of the Octopus Publishing Group
Michelin House
81 Fulham Road
London SW3 6RB

© Cathay Books 1981
ISBN 0 7064 3841 8

Printed by Mandarin Offset in Hong Kong

INTRODUCTION

This book shows you some of the different ways of preserving fruits and vegetables. Making preserves is a process which cannot be hurried and a skill to be used through the year as ingredients come into season. At the beginning of each chapter are a few general guidelines which should be followed for success. The following notes apply to all the recipes in the book.

Flavourings: The herbs and spices chosen can be varied and increased or decreased in quantity to suit tastes.

Sugar: The amount can be varied to taste in pickles and chutneys but not in jams, jellies, conserves, marmalades, cheeses and curds. Granulated, preserving or cube sugars are equally suitable for all the recipes unless a certain type of sugar is specified.

Equipment: Heavy-based, large, wide preserving pans or saucepans reduce the risk of thick mixtures sticking or burning. They should be no more than one third full so that the contents can be boiled rapidly after the sugar has been added, without the danger of boiling over. Long-handled wooden spoons for stirring, and a perforated spoon for removing scum are very useful. A sugar thermometer takes the guesswork out of setting points and is used when bottling fruits and sterilizing sauces and syrups. Nylon jelly bags are easier and quicker to use and more readily available than felt or flannel ones.

Sterilizing jars and bottles: Wash them well, rinse in hot water and invert to drain. Just before filling, put into a cool oven, 140°C (275°F), Gas Mark 1, to sterilize and become hot so they will not crack when filled. Jars and bottles must be sterilized for *all* preserves.

Storage: Unless otherwise specified, all the pickles and preserves in this book can be kept for at least a year. However for optimum flavour it's wise to use them within the year, before the following season's replacements are ready. Store in a cool, dry dark place.

NOTES
Standard spoon measurements are used in all recipes
1 tablespoon = one 15 ml spoon
1 teaspoon = one 5 ml spoon
All spoon measurements are level.

Fresh herbs are used unless otherwise stated. Use freshly ground black pepper where pepper is specified.

For all recipes, quantities are given in both metric and imperial measures. Follow either set but not a mixture of both, because they are not interchangeable.

JAMS AND JELLIES

These are made by boiling fruit or fruit juices with sugar until the sugar and pectin combine in such a way that the mixture will set lightly when cold. Pectin, a natural gum-like substance, is present in different fruits in different quantities; it is released when fruit is simmered with acid.

Fruits containing sufficient pectin and acid, such as cooking apples, currants, damsons, gooseberries and some plums, make a good setting jam. Others, like apricots, blackberries, greengages, loganberries and raspberries, containing less acid have medium setting properties and additional acid is usually added for setting. Cherries, pears, rhubarb and some varieties of strawberries are low in pectin and difficult to set without the addition of homemade or commercial pectin (called pectin stock in this book); alternatively, they can be mixed with fruits rich in pectin and acid.

JAMS

Fruit must be fresh and slightly under-ripe. Wash, if necessary, and drain very well. Prepare in the usual way.

Pectin is extracted by simmering the fruit in a little water until soft. If additional acid is needed (see left), add 2 tablespoons lemon juice or $\frac{1}{2}$ teaspoon citric acid or tartaric acid to each 1.75 kg (4 lb) fruit.

Test for pectin: Put 1 teaspoon juice from the pan into a small glass. Leave until cold, then add 3 teaspoons methylated spirit. Shake gently and leave for 1 minute. A jelly-like lump indicates plenty of pectin present and up to 750 g (1$\frac{1}{2}$ lb) sugar can be added for each 500 g (1 lb) fruit; 2 or 3 less firm clots shows moderate pectin and 500 g (1 lb) sugar can be added for each 500 g (1 lb) fruit. The more sugar you can add, the greater the yield will be, without affecting the sweetness of the jam.

Lots of small clots indicates little pectin and the jam is unlikely to set unless pectin stock or another high pectin fruit is added. When commercial pectin stock is added, follow the manufacturer's directions. If homemade pectin stock is added (see page 8), use 60–120 ml (2–4 fl oz) to 500 g (1 lb) fruit.

Sugar: Heat the sugar in a cool oven, 140°C (275°F), Gas Mark 1, before adding to the pan; it will then dissolve more quickly.

Test for setting: This can be done in three ways.

By temperature: Boil to 104°C (220°F), using a sugar thermometer to check the temperature.

By weight: Before starting, weigh the empty pan; weigh again when the jam is cooked. Subtract the weight of the empty pan from this to give the weight of the jam. For each 1.5 kg (3 lb) sugar added there should be 2.25 kg (5 lb) finished jam.

Saucer test: Cool 1 teaspoon jam on a saucer. A skin should form which wrinkles when pushed with a finger.

Potting: Remove the jam from the heat and skim off any scum with a perforated spoon. Pour immediately into hot sterilized jars (see page 5), filling to the brim.

If the jam contains whole fruit, cool it in the pan until a skin forms and the fruit begins to sink, then stir carefully; this spreads the fruit evenly. Pot as above.

Cover the surface immediately with waxed discs, wax side down, leaving no space between the discs and the jam. Top with a cellophane or other suitable cover while very hot or when quite cold. Label when cold.

JELLIES

As the pulp is discarded, choose fruit with a good flavour. Apple can be added to help the setting.

Pectin: Simmer the fruit in water until very soft. For each 500 g (1 lb) soft fruit use 150 ml ($\frac{1}{4}$ pint) water and for each 500 g (1 lb) hard fruit use up to 450 ml ($\frac{3}{4}$ pint). The more water you can add the greater the yield will be. Strain the cooked fruit through a jelly bag; do not squeeze or the jelly will be cloudy.

Test for pectin: Put 1 teaspoon juice from the pan into a small glass. Leave until cold, then add 3 teaspoons methylated spirit. Shake gently and leave for 1 minute. A jelly-like lump indicates plenty of pectin present. If a firm clot is not obtained continue simmering to evaporate more water. If the clot is *very* firm, simmer the pulp with half the original volume of water, strain and mix the two liquids together. For each 600 ml (1 pint) strained juice add 500 g (1 lb) sugar.

Potting: Finish as for jam, using small jars.

PECTIN STOCK

This is usually prepared from cooking apples, cut up without peeling or coring, but gooseberries or redcurrants can also be used.

Put 600 ml (1 pint) water and 1 kg (2 lb) fruit in a pan, bring slowly to the boil, then simmer for about 1 hour until the fruit is very soft. Test for pectin (see above). If a firm clot is not obtained, simmer a little longer. Strain.

Bring the strained juice to the boil and pour into hot sterilized preserving jars (see page 5). Sterilize as for Method 2 of Fruit Bottling (see page 42), simmering for 5 minutes. Use within 4 months.

Harmony Jam

500 g (1 lb) dessert
  apples
750 g (1½ lb) cooking
  pears, peeled,
  core and diced
250 g (8 oz) red
  plums, stoned and
  quartered
250 ml (8 fl oz)
  cold water
1.25 kg (2½ lb) sugar
  (approximately)

Peel and core the apples. Place the peel and cores on a square of muslin and tie loosely. Cut the flesh into small pieces.

Put all the fruit, the muslin bag and the water in a pan. Cook gently for about 20 minutes until the fruit is soft.

Test for pectin. When a firm clot is obtained, remove the muslin bag and squeeze out all the liquid.

Add the sugar (see page 7). Stir until dissolved, then boil rapidly, stirring occasionally, until setting point is reached. Cool slightly, then stir and pour into hot sterilized jars; cover.

Makes about 1.75–2 kg (4–4½ lb)

Green Gooseberry Jam

Gooseberry jam is often red in colour but it can be kept green.
Choose a variety which tends to stay green when stewed and
make sure the fruit is slightly under-ripe. It helps to use a
copper or brass pan. Make sure there is a firm pectin clot
before adding the sugar, because prolonged boiling after the
sugar has been added changes the colour.

1 kg (2 lb) green
   gooseberries, topped
   and tailed
450 ml (¾ pint) water
1.5 kg (3 lb) sugar
   (approximately)

Put the gooseberries in a pan with the
water and simmer until the fruit is very
soft. Test for pectin and when a firm
clot is obtained, add the sugar (see
page 7) and stir until dissolved. Bring
to the boil and boil rapidly until setting
point is reached, stirring occasionally.
Remove any scum. Cool slightly, stir
and pour into hot serilized jars; cover.
Makes about 2.25 kg (5 lb)
NOTE: If the variety of fruit used does
not give a firm clot, boil for 3 minutes
after the sugar has dissolved, then add
175 ml (6 fl oz) commercial or homemade pectin stock (see page 8).
Remove from the heat and leave for
5 minutes then stir and pot.
   To give a muscatel flavour to this
jam, tie up 12 heads of elder flowers in
muslin and cook with the fruit.
Remove before the sugar is added.

Strawberry Jam

We expect to find whole strawberries in strawberry jam, but
to extract enough pectin to make a set, the fruit must be
cooked until it is broken down. The alternative is to add
commercial or homemade pectin stock. Some varieties of
strawberry are also short of acid; in this recipe, orange juice is
added to ensure there is sufficient, but it is not essential.

1 kg (2 lb) small
   whole strawberries,
   hulled
1.5 kg (3 lb) sugar
juice of 1 orange
175 ml (6 fl oz)
   pectin stock (see
   page 8)

Put the strawberries in a pan with the
sugar and orange juice. Heat gently,
stirring occasionally, until the sugar
has dissolved, bring to the boil and
simmer for 5 minutes. Remove from
the heat and stir in the pectin stock.
Cool for 10 to 15 minutes, then stir.
Pour into hot sterilized jars and cover.
Makes about 1.75 kg (4 lb)

Spiced Plum Jam with Walnuts

1.75 kg (4 lb) plums,
    halved and stoned
450 ml (¾ pint)
    cold water
5 cm (2 inch) piece of
    cinnamon stick
1.5 kg (3 lb) sugar
    (approximately)
75 g (3 oz) walnuts,
    finely chopped

Put the plums in a pan with the water and cinnamon. Simmer until the fruit is very soft. Test for pectin.

When a satisfactory clot is obtained, remove the cinnamon, add the sugar (see page 7) and stir until dissolved. Bring to the boil and boil rapidly until setting point is reached, stirring occasionally. Remove any scum, cool slightly, then stir in the walnuts. Pour into hot sterilized jars and cover.

Makes about 2.75 kg (6 lb)

Apricot Jam with Brandy

1.5 kg (3 lb) apricots
450 ml (¾ pint) cold
　　water
juice of 2 lemons
1.5 kg (3 lb) sugar
　　(approximately)
175 ml (6 fl oz)
　　apricot brandy or
　　brandy

Halve the apricots and remove the stones. Crack one third of the stones and remove the kernels; blanch by dipping into hot water to remove the skins.

Put the apricots, kernels, water and lemon juice in a pan and simmer until the fruit is tender. Test for pectin.

When a satisfactory clot is formed, add the sugar (see page 7), stir until dissolved, then bring to the boil and boil rapidly until setting point is reached, stirring occasionally. Remove from the heat and immediately stir in the brandy. Remove any scum, pour into hot sterilized jars and cover.

Makes about 2.25 kg (5 lb)

Blackcurrant Jam

This is an example of a jam so naturally rich in both pectin and acid that a high proportion of sugar can be added – 750 g (1½ lb) to 500 g (1 lb) of fruit.

1 kg (2 lb) black-
currants, stalks
removed
600 ml (1 pint) water
1.5 kg (3½ lb) sugar
(approximately)

Put the blackcurrants and water in a pan, bring to the boil and simmer gently until the fruit is soft and pulpy. (The skins will toughen if the fruit is cooked too quickly.) Test for pectin: it should give a very firm clot; if not, simmer a little longer.

Add the sugar (see page 7), stir until dissolved, then boil rapidly until setting point is reached, stirring occasionally. Cool slightly, then stir. Pour into hot sterilized jars and cover.

Makes about 2.25 kg (5 lb)

Rhubarb and Orange Jam

1.5 kg (3 lb) rhubarb,
   cut into 2.5 cm
   (1 inch) lengths
1.5 kg (3 lb) sugar
grated rind and
   juice of 1 lemon
2 thin-skinned
   oranges

Put alternate layers of rhubarb and sugar in a bowl. Add the lemon rind and juice, cover and leave for 24 hours.

Next day, boil the oranges in 600 ml (1 pint) water for about 1 hour or until translucent; drain. Cut 5 thin slices from the oranges, discarding any pips. Cut the remaining oranges into small pieces and add to the rhubarb; stir well. Place in a pan, bring slowly to the boil, stirring until the sugar has dissolved, then boil rapidly until setting point is reached, stirring occasionally.

Cool slightly, then remove any scum. Stir again and quarter-fill five 500 g (1 lb) hot sterilized jars. Carefully slide an orange slice down the side of each jar. Fill carefully, without displacing the orange, and cover.

Makes about 2.25 kg (5 lb)

Uncooked Raspberry Jam

This jam has a gorgeous flavour and will keep for up to
2 months. No other fruit can be used in this way.

1 kg (2 lb) ripe
*   raspberries*
1 kg (2 lb) sugar
a little brandy

Put the raspberries and sugar, in
separate bowls, in a preheated moderate
oven, 180°C (350°F), Gas Mark 4, for
about 20 minutes or until they are both
really hot. Add the sugar to the raspberries and beat the two together until
the sugar has dissolved. Pour into small
hot sterilized jars and leave to cool.

Brush a little brandy on the waxed
side of each jam cover and finish in
the usual way.

Makes about 1.75 kg (4 lb)

NOTE: If larger quantities of fruit and
sugar are put into the bowls, increase
the heating time to 30 minutes.

Redcurrant Jelly

Currants, if not over-ripe, are rich in pectin, so more water can be added to them than many other fruits to give a greater yield. A mixture of red and white currants can be used. Blackcurrant jelly is made in the same way.

1 kg (2 lb)
  redcurrants
900 ml (1½ pints)
  water
750 g (1½ lb) sugar
  (approximately)

Remove any leaves from the fruit, but leave the stalks on. Put in a pan with the water, heat slowly and simmer until tender. Mash with a wooden spoon and strain through a jelly bag. Test the juice for pectin; it should form a firm clot.

Put in a pan and add the sugar (see page 8). Heat gently, stirring, until the sugar has dissolved, then boil rapidly until setting point is reached, stirring occasionally. Pour into small, hot sterilized jars and cover.
Makes about 1.5 kg (3 lb)

Sweet Pepper Jelly

500 g (1 lb) large red
  peppers, cored and
  seeded
500 g (1 lb) large green
  peppers, cored and
  seeded
1.25 kg (2½ lb) sugar
150 ml (¼ pint) cider
  vinegar
150 ml (¼ pint)
  lemon juice
175 ml (6 fl oz) pectin
  stock (see page 8)

Put the peppers in an electric blender and blend until very finely chopped, or mince twice, collecting the juices. Put in a large pan with the sugar and vinegar. Bring to the boil, stirring until the sugar has dissolved. Remove from the heat and set aside for 30 to 45 minutes.

Add the lemon juice and bring back to the boil, stirring frequently. Boil rapidly for 2 minutes.

Stir in the pectin stock and strain through a nylon jelly bag or 2 thick-nesses of muslin in a sieve. Collect in a heated bowl, skim, pour into small, hot sterilized jars and cover.

Serve this delicious, unusual jelly with cold meats, especially lamb and chicken, as well as prawns and cream cheese.
Makes about 1.5 kg (3 lb)
NOTE: Do not use a thick flannel or felt jelly bag or the jelly will begin to set before it has all run through.

Bramble Jelly

500 g (1 lb) cooking
  apples or windfalls
1.25 kg (2½ lb)
  blackberries
600 ml (1 pint) water
1 kg (2 lb) sugar
  (approximately)

Cut the apples into pieces, without peeling or coring. Put in a pan with the blackberries and water. Bring to the boil and simmer until the fruit is very soft. Mash with a wooden spoon and strain through a jelly bag. Test the juice for pectin; it should form a firm clot.

Put in a pan and add the sugar (see page 8). Heat gently, stirring, until dissolved, then boil rapidly until setting point is reached, stirring occasionally. Pour into small, hot sterilized jars and cover while hot.

Makes about 1.5 kg (3 lb)

NOTE: The proportions of fruit can be altered. If more apple (which contains most pectin) is used, the proportion of sugar can be increased to give a greater yield, but the flavour will be reduced.

Ripe elderberries can replace the blackberries; use equal quantities of apples and elderberries.

Apple Jelly

Apple jelly is quite pleasant plain, especially with hot, buttered scones. Add herbs and it becomes a delicious jelly to serve with hot and cold fish, meat and poultry dishes.

1.75 kg (4 lb)
cooking apples
1.75 litres (3 pints)
cold water
750 g (1½ lb) sugar
(approximately)

Cut up the apples, discarding any bruised parts. Put in a pan with the water and bring to the boil, then simmer until very soft. Mash with a wooden spoon and strain through a jelly bag. Test the juice for pectin; it should form a firm clot.

Put in a pan and add the sugar (see page 8). Heat gently, stirring, until dissolved, then boil rapidly until setting point is reached, stirring occasionally. Remove any scum, pour into small, hot sterilized jars and cover.

Makes about 1.5 kg (3½ lb)

Variations
Some of these jellies, particularly the rosemary and mint ones, can be melted and poured over ice cream or added to fruit salads.

Sage Jelly: Add 4 tablespoons chopped sage after removing from the heat.

Rosemary Jelly: Add 8 large rosemary sprigs with the water. Set a further sprig in each pot.

Dill Jelly: Add 4 tablespoons chopped dill or 2 tablespoons dried dill weed after removing from heat.

Thyme Jelly: Add 8 large thyme sprigs with the water. Set a further sprig in each jar.

Mint Jelly: Add a small bunch of mint with the water. Add 6–8 tablespoons chopped mint after removing from heat.

Bouquet Garni Jelly: Tie 1 parsley sprig, 2 bay leaves and 1 small thyme sprig with a length of sterilized kitchen string. Put one in each jar of jelly.

MARMALADES

Marmalade, originally made from bitter or Seville oranges, is now made from all varieties of oranges, grapefruit, lemons and limes, including tangerines, satsumas and ugli fruit, on their own or in various combinations. Flavourings such as ginger, whisky, treacle and apricot can be added, but the citrus flavour must predominate.

Marmalade-making is very similar to jam-making, but the rind needs much longer cooking so more water is required. The fruit is simmered until the rind is soft and the volume of liquid has reduced by about half. Jelly marmalades are made in the same way, but they are strained through a jelly bag after the fruit has been cooked and strips of rind are then added.

Pectin is contained in the white pith and pips. Extra acid is often added to ensure a good set, as only about 500 g (1 lb) fruit is used to make 1.5 kg (3 lb) marmalade. Test for pectin as for jellies (see page 8).

Fruit: Always wash the fruit thoroughly (as it is often sprayed in the orchards), scrubbing the skins if at all dirty.

Halve the fruit, squeeze out the juice and reserve the pips. Remove the white pith from the rind and cut it up

roughly. Place on a square of muslin with the pips and tie loosely. When removing from the pan, squeeze the bag well to extract all the liquid.

Shred the rind finely for a medium thick marmalade. A thicker, chunkier marmalade can be made by leaving all or part of the pith with the rind and preparing in a cutting machine or a mincer.

Sugar: Weigh the pan when empty. When the pectin test is satisfactory, weigh the pulp in the pan. Subtract the weight of the empty pan from this to obtain the weight of the pulp. For each 500 g (1 lb) pulp weight, add 500 g (1 lb) sugar. Heat the sugar as for jam (see page 7) before adding to the pulp.

Setting point: Once the sugar has dissolved, marmalade should be boiled very fast to reach setting point quickly. If it takes longer than 15 to 20 minutes the marmalade will darken and lose its fresh flavour. Test for setting as for jam (see page 7).

Potting: Remove the marmalade from the heat and skim off any scum immediately with a perforated spoon or it may stick to the rind and cloud the marmalade. Leave to stand for a few minutes until a skin forms and the rind begins to sink. Stir and pour into hot sterilized jars (see page 5).

Bitter Orange Marmalade

1 kg (2 lb) Seville
   oranges
juice from 1 lemon
2.25 litres (4 pints)
   cold water
2.75 kg (6 lb) sugar
   (approximately)

Prepare the fruit, pith and pips. Place in a weighed pan and add the lemon juice and water. Bring to the boil and simmer for 2 hours or until reduced by about half and the rind is tender.

Test for pectin. When a firm clot is obtained, remove the muslin bag.

Weigh the pulp and add the sugar (see page 21). Heat gently, stirring, until dissolved, then bring to the boil and boil rapidly until setting point is reached.

Remove from the heat, skim off any scum and leave for a few minutes. Stir again and pour into hot sterilized jars. Put on the waxed discs immediately. Cover when cold.
Makes about 4.5 kg (10 lb)

Whisky Marmalade: Make as above, adding 2 tablespoons whisky for each 500 g (1 lb) marmalade just before setting point is reached.

Mixed Fruit Marmalade

Any combination of citrus fruits can be used, though the most usual combination is sweet oranges, lemons and grapefruits.

1.5 kg (3 lb) mixed citrus fruits
3.5 litres (6 pints) cold water
2.75 kg (6 lb) sugar

Prepare the fruit, pith and pips and put in a weighed pan with the water. Bring to the boil and simmer for about 2 hours, until reduced by about half and the rind is tender.

Test for pectin. When a firm clot is obtained, remove the muslin bag. Weigh the pulp and add the sugar (see page 21). Heat gently, stirring, until dissolved, then bring to the boil and boil rapidly until setting point is reached.

Remove from the heat, skim off any scum and leave for a few minutes. Stir again and pour into hot sterilized jars. Put in the waxed discs immediately. Cover when cold.

Makes about 4.5 kg (10 lb)

Orange and Peach Marmalade

8 thin-skinned oranges
juice of 1 lemon
900 ml (1½ pints)
    cold water
4 peaches, skinned,
    stoned and sliced
750 g (1½ lb) sugar
    (approximately)

Cut the oranges into quarters. Remove the pips, place on a square of muslin and tie loosely.

Mince the oranges and put in a weighed pan with the orange and lemon juice, water and muslin bag. Simmer for 1½ hours or until the rind is very soft.

Add the peaches and cook for 5 minutes. Test for pectin. When a firm clot is obtained, remove the muslin bag. Weigh the pulp and add 350 g (12 oz) sugar to each 500 g (1 lb) pulp.

Heat gently, stirring, until the sugar has dissolved, then boil rapidly until setting point is reached.

Remove from the heat, skim off any scum and cool slightly. Stir again, pour into hot sterilized jars and put in the waxed discs. Cover when cold.
Makes about 3 kg (7 lb)

Ginger Marmalade

1 kg (2 lb) grapefruit
250 g (8 oz) lemons
2.75 litres (5 pints)
    cold water
2.25 kg (5 lb)
    demerara or
    granulated sugar
    (approximately)
150 g (5 oz) preserved
    ginger, finely
    chopped

Prepare the fruit, pith and pips. Put in a weighed pan with the water. Bring to the boil and simmer for about 2 hours, until reduced by about half and the rind is tender.

Test for pectin. When a firm clot is obtained, discard the muslin bag. Weigh the pulp and add the sugar (see page 21) and ginger.

Heat gently, stirring, until the sugar has dissolved, then boil rapidly until setting point is reached.

Remove from the heat and skim off any scum; extra care must be taken if using demerara sugar as this forms more scum. Leave for a few minutes.

Stir again and pour into hot sterilized jars. Put in the waxed discs immediately. Cover when cold.

Serve this marmalade at tea-time, or use as a cake filling or a ginger sauce.
Makes about 3.5 kg (8 lb)

Lemon or Lime Marmalade

8 large ripe lemons
   or 16 medium ripe
   limes
2.25 litres (4 pints)
   cold water
1.75 kg (4 lb) sugar
   (approximately)

Remove the rinds with a potato peeler and cut into fine shreds. Remove the white pith and place on a square of muslin. If using lemons, add the pips to the pith; if using limes, discard the pips. Tie loosely. Chop the flesh finely.

Put the rind, flesh and any juice, muslin bag and water in a weighed pan. Bring to the boil and simmer for about 2 hours, until reduced by about half and the rind is tender.

Test for pectin. When a firm clot is obtained, discard the muslin bag. Weigh the pulp and add the sugar (see page 21). Heat gently, stirring, until dissolved, then bring to the boil and boil rapidly until setting point is reached.

Remove from the heat and skim off any scum. Leave for a few minutes, stir again and pour into hot sterilized jars. Put in the waxed discs immediately. Cover when cold.

Makes about 2.75 kg (6 lb)

Orange Jelly Marmalade

1 kg (2 lb) Seville
    oranges
juice of 1 lemon
2.25 litres (4 pints)
    cold water
1.75 kg (4 lb) sugar
    (approximately)

Halve the fruit and squeeze out the juice into a weighed pan, reserving the pips. Remove the pith from enough rind to give 50 g (2 oz) rind from each 500 g (1 lb) fruit. Shred this rind finely, place on a square of muslin with the pips and tie loosely. Add to the pan. Cut up the remaining pith and rind and add to the pan with the lemon juice and water.

Bring to the boil and simmer for about 2 hours; remove the muslin bag after 1½ hours to prevent the rind becoming too soft: keep on one side.

Strain through a jelly bag and test the juice for pectin; it should form a firm clot. Put in a pan and add the sugar (see page 8) and the strips of rind removed from the muslin bag.

Heat gently, stirring, until the sugar had dissolved, then bring to the boil and boil rapidly until setting point is reached.

Remove from the heat, skim off any scum, and leave to stand for a few minutes. Stir again and pour into hot sterilized jars. Put in the waxed discs immediately. Cover when cold.

Makes about 2.75 kg (6 lb)

FRUIT CHEESES, CURDS AND MINCEMEAT

FRUIT CHEESES
The fruits used for jams and jellies can also be used for making fruit cheeses, but a larger amount of fruit is needed to produce the same weight of the finished product. The fruits used must be strongly flavoured.

Fruit cheeses are best set in small dishes or moulds which have been lightly brushed with glycerine so they can be turned out to serve. They can also be set in small jars. Whichever type of container is used, it must be sterilized (see page 5) and covered immediately as for jam (see page 8).

Fruit cheeses can be served in place of cheese or, cut into small pieces, as a sweetmeat. They can be stored for up to 4 months.

FRUIT CURDS
These rich preserves are a mixture of butter, eggs and sugar with a flavouring of fruit pulp or juice. They require constant attention during cooking, as the mixture will curdle if it is boiled. To avoid this, they can be cooked in a double boiler or in a basin standing over a pan of hot water; the cooking time will, of course, be longer.

The same rules apply for sterilizing jars (see page 5); pot as for jam (see page 8). They can be stored for up to 1 month in a cool dark place, 2 to 3 months in a refrigerator.

Apple and Raspberry Cheese

750 g (1½ lb) cooking
   apples
500 g (1 lb)
   raspberries
1.5 kg (3 lb) sugar
   (approximately)
red food colouring
   (optional)

Cut up the apples, without peeling or coring, and put in a pan with just enough water to cover the base. Cover and cook very gently, stirring occasionally, until soft. Add the raspberries and cook, uncovered, until they can be mashed to a pulp.

Rub through a nylon or hair sieve and weigh the resulting pulp. Return to the pan and cook carefully until the purée is as thick as possible.

Add 500 g (1 lb) sugar for each 500 g (1 lb) pulp. Stir until dissolved, then cook slowly until a wooden spoon pulled along the base of the pan leaves a clear line. Stir in a little red food colouring, if using.

Pour into prepared containers and cover immediately.

Makes about 1 kg (2 lb)

Damson Cheese

1.25 kg (2½ lb)
   damsons, stoned
150 ml (¼ pint) water
1 kg (2 lb) sugar
   (approximately)

Put the damsons in a pan with the water. Bring to the boil, cover and simmer until very soft. Rub through a nylon or hair sieve and weigh the resulting pulp. Return to the pan and cook carefully until the purée is as thick as possible.

Add 500 g (1 lb) sugar for each 500 g (1 lb) pulp. Stir until dissoved. then cook slowly until a wooden spoon pulled along the base of the pan leaves a clear line.

Pour into prepared containers and cover immediately.

Makes about 750 g (1½ lb)

NOTE: If liked, crack the damson stones and add a few skinned kernels to each jar before covering.

Banana Curd

4 large bananas
125 g (4 oz) butter
250 g (8 oz) caster
* sugar*
grated rind and juice
* of 1 lemon*
4 eggs

Mash the bananas, using a wooden fork or spoon. Melt the butter slowly in a heavy-based pan, then add the sugar, bananas, lemon rind and juice. Cook for 10 minutes.

Beat the eggs with a wooden spoon, then gradually beat in 3 tablespoons of the banana mixture; this prevents the eggs curdling.

Pour onto the remaining banana mixture, stirring. Cook gently, stirring constantly, until the mixture is thick enough to coat the back of the spoon; do not boil.

Pour into hot sterilized jars and cover.

Makes about 1 kg (2 lb)

Scottish Curd

3 large lemons
175 g (6 oz) unsalted
  butter
500 g (1 lb) sugar
4 medium eggs,
  beaten
3 tablespoons
  Drambuie

Grate the coloured rind from the lemons using a fine grater. Melt the butter slowly in a heavy-based pan and stir in the lemon rind and sugar. Heat gently until the sugar has dissolved. Do not stir.

Stir 1 tablespoon of the hot mixture into the eggs; repeat twice more; this prevents the eggs curdling.

Pour into the pan and heat gently, stirring, until the mixture thickens and coats the back of a wooden spoon. Stir in the Drambuie and heat until thick again; do not boil. Pour into hot sterilized jars and cover.

Makes about 750 g (1½ lb)

Mincemeat

1 kg (2 lb) cooking
   apples, peeled,
   cored and grated
350 g (12 oz) carrots,
   grated
250 g (8 oz) cut
   mixed peel
750 g (1½ lb) currants
750 g (1½ lb) sultanas
350 g (12 oz) shredded
   suet
750 g (1½ lb) granulated
   or soft brown sugar
50 g (2 oz) almonds,
   skinned and chopped
1½ teaspoons ground
   mixed spice
1 teaspoon grated
   nutmeg
150 ml (¼ pint)
   brandy or rum

Put all the ingredients, except the
brandy or rum, into a large basin and
mix well. Cover and leave for 24 hours,
then add the spirit and mix again.
Pack into sterilized jars and cover.
   If it is to be kept for more than a
few weeks, seal with an airtight cover
as for pickles (see page 47).
Makes about 4 kg (9 lb)

Orange Curd

250 g (8 oz) sugar
   cubes
3 oranges
125 g (4 oz) unsalted
   butter
5 medium eggs,
   beaten

Rub the sugar cubes against the rind
of the oranges until they are well
coloured and have absorbed all the zest.
   Squeeze the juice from the oranges:
there should be 400 ml (14 fl oz); if
necessary, squeeze another orange to
get this amount of juice.
   Melt the butter slowly in a heavy-
based pan, then stir in the sugar and
orange juice. Heat gently until the
sugar has dissolved.
   Stir 1 tablespoon of the hot mixture
into the beaten eggs. Repeat twice
more; this prevents the eggs curdling.
   Pour into the pan and heat gently,
stirring, until the mixture thickens and
coats the back of a wooden spoon; do
not boil. Pour into hot sterilized jars
and cover.
Makes about 750 g (1½ lb)
NOTE: Lemon curd can be made in the
same way.

33

CONSERVES

In conserves the fruit stays whole, or the size into which it is cut, and is suspended in a syrup which does not set as stiffly as in normal jams. The same basic rules apply as for jam-making: test for setting point (see page 7), sterilize jars (see page 5), pot and cover as for jam (see page 8).

Conserves are delicious to eat, not only with bread and butter or scones, but used as a sauce on ice creams, hot sponge puddings or milk puddings, and of course as a filling for sponges or gâteaux. They are often flavoured with brandy or other alcohol and make acceptable gifts.

As conserves are richer than jams, they have a shorter shelf life and should be used within 6 months.

Fig Conserve

1 kg (2 lb) green
  figs, quartered
2 lemons
1 kg (2 lb) sugar

Put the figs in a pan with the finely grated rind and the juice of the lemons and cook gently until soft. If necessary, add 2 tablespoons water.

Meanwhile, warm the sugar in a bowl in a preheated moderate oven, 180°C (350°F), Gas Mark 4, for 20 minutes.

Add the sugar to the figs and heat gently, stirring, until dissolved, then bring to the boil and boil rapidly until setting point is reached. Cool slightly, stir, then pour into hot sterilized jars and cover.
Makes about 1.75 kg (4 lb)

Peach Conserve with Brandy

750 g (1½ lb) fully
  ripe peaches
50 g (2 oz) slivered
  almonds
40 g (1½ oz) glacé
  cherries
½ teaspoon finely
  grated lemon rind
1 tablespoon lemon
  juice
small pinch of
  ground cinnamon
625 g (1¼ lb) sugar
3 tablespoons brandy
120 ml (4 fl oz) pectin
  stock (see page 8)

Peel, stone and cut the peaches into pieces the size of raspberries, collecting all the juice. Place in a pan with the almonds, cherries, lemon rind and juice and cinnamon. Bring to the boil, stirring occasionally.

Add the sugar and bring to a full, rolling boil, stirring until the sugar has dissolved. Remove from the heat and stir in the brandy and pectin stock.

Leave to stand for 5 minutes then stir again. Pour into hot sterilized jars and cover.

Makes about 1.25 kg (2½ lb)

Black Cherry Conserve

Black cherries are deficient in pectin and acid so redcurrant juice is added to obtain a satisfactory set; it also provides additional flavour.

625 g (1¼ lb) black
  cherries, stoned
500 g (1 lb) sugar
150 ml (¼ pint) water
500 g (1 lb) redcurrants
3 tablespoons brandy
  (optional)

Place the cherries in a basin. Put the sugar and water in a pan and heat gently, stirring until dissolved, then bring to the boil. Pour immediately over the cherries, cover and leave for 24 hours

Cook the redcurrants in just enough water to prevent them sticking until soft. Mash and strain through a nylon jelly bag; there should be 150 ml (¼ pint).

Transfer the cherries and juice to a pan. Add the redcurrant juice and bring to the boil. Simmer for 10 minutes or until the cherries are soft. Transfer to hot sterilized jars, using a slotted spoon. Boil the juice until setting point is reached, then skim off the scum.

Stir in the brandy, if using. Pour over the cherries and cover.

Makes about 1–1.25 kg (2–2½ lb)
NOTE: 175 ml (6 fl oz) pectin stock may be used in place of the redcurrant juice. Add to the conserve juice after removing the cherries.

Strawberry Conserve

Use very small, slightly under-ripe berries.

1 kg (2 lb) very small
*   strawberries*
1 kg (2 lb) sugar
juice of ½ lemon

Put alternate layers of strawberries and sugar in a basin. Add the lemon juice, cover and leave to stand for 24 hours.

Transfer the fruit and sugar to a pan, bring slowly to the boil and simmer for 5 minutes. Pour back into the basin and leave for another 24 hours.

Transfer to a pan, bring to the boil and simmer until setting point is reached. Remove from the heat and leave to cool a little until the fruit begins to sink in the syrup. Stir and pour into small, hot sterilized jars. Cover immediately.

Makes about 1.5 kg (3 lb)

37

Stuffed Oranges Supreme

For this conserve, use small, wide-mouthed preserving jars.

6 seedless oranges
(Navel or
Valencia), about
6 cm (2½ inches) in
diameter
350 g (12 oz) sugar
175 g (6 oz) golden
syrup
4 tablespoons syrup
from maraschino
cherries
50 g (2 oz) maraschino
cherries, chopped
125 g (4 oz) stoned
dates, chopped
50 g (2 oz) walnuts,
chopped
25 g (1 oz) candied
ginger, chopped

Wash the oranges well, cover with cold water and leave overnight.

Cut off the stem end of each orange and reserve. Scoop out as much flesh as possible and set aside. Soak the orange shells and tops in 600 ml (1 pint) cold water or water to cover for 2 hours. Drain, reserving the liquid.

Put the sugar, golden syrup, reserved water and cherry syrup in a pan and bring to the boil.

Mix together the cherries, dates, walnuts and ginger and use to fill the oranges, packing firmly. Replace the lids and secure with cocktail sticks.

Add the orange flesh to the syrup. Put the oranges on top, in a single layer. Simmer for 45 minutes or until the oranges are translucent. Pack the oranges in 3 hot sterilized preserving jars.

Strain the syrup, return to the pan and bring to a rapid boil. Pour over the oranges, filling the jars to the top. Cover and seal.

Cut into thin wedges and serve with roast duckling or pork, or serve in their syrup with ice cream or fruit.
Makes about 1 kg (2 lb)

Grape Conserve with Port

500 g (1 lb) seedless
green grapes
500 g (1 lb) sugar
450 ml (¾ pint)
port wine

Remove any stalks and put the grapes in a pan with the sugar and port. Heat gently, stirring until the sugar has dissolved, then boil carefully, stirring frequently, until the grapes are soft and the syrup very thick.

Pour into small, hot sterilized jars and cover with an airtight seal as for pickles (see page 47).
Makes about 625 g (1¼ lb)

BOTTLING

This is a way of preserving fruit, usually in syrup. The fruit is heated in special jars to destroy yeasts and moulds naturally present on fruit, and to form an airtight seal to prevent more entering. Simple rules are applied to all methods of preserving. Only fruit, not vegetables, can be preserved this way; tomatoes are, botanically, fruits.

Vacuum Bottles and Jars: English Kilner jars are available in 500 ml (17.5 fl oz), 1 litre (35 fl oz) and 1.5 litre (52.5 fl oz) sizes. Imported jars are available in other sizes.

Screw-top jars have rubber rings to separate the top rims from glass or metal tops. They are fitted with plastic or metal screw bands which are tightened during cooling to help form a vacuum.

Clip jars also have rubber rings to separate the top rims from metal or glass tops, but they are fitted with metal spring clips. These allow steam and air to escape but no air can re-enter.

Jam jars can be fitted with special covers with rubber rings and clips made specially for them, or a special preserving skin available from chemists can be used. These are less likely to be as satisfactory as the other types.

Preparation: Before use, examine the tops of the jars and the lids to ensure there is no chip or crack to prevent a vacuum. Stretch rubber rings a little to make sure they are elastic enough to return to their original size. Sterilize jars and lids (see page 5). Soak rubber rings in cold water for 10 minutes, then dip into boiling water before using.

Fruit: Should be as perfect as possible and slightly under-ripe. Prepare as necessary, removing stones if possible as these may alter the flavour of the fruit during storage.

Syrup: Sugar syrup gives the best flavour, but honey or golden syrup can also be used. See chart (page 44) for quantities. Put the sugar and water in a pan and heat gently,

stirring, until dissolved, then boil for 1 minute. If it is to be used cold, use only half the water with the sugar, then add iced water to bring to the correct strength.

For additional flavour, whole spices, strips of fruit rind, etc. can be added to the sugar; the syrup is then strained before use. Spirits, liqueurs, port, ginger syrup, etc. can be added to the sugar syrup.

Packing the Fruit: Pack the fruit into the jars as tightly as possible as it will shrink a little during heating; a chopstick or similar utensil is useful for positioning it. Add the syrup gradually, banging the jar lightly on several thicknesses of cloth (to avoid breaking) with each addition to remove air bubbles.

Bottling Tomatoes: Tomatoes are best skinned. Small ones can be left whole and bottled in brine, using 1 tablespoon salt to 1.2 litres (2 pints) water. Larger ones should be halved or quartered and packed tightly (solid pack) with 1 teaspoon salt and 2 teaspoons sugar to each 500 g (1 lb). For all tomatoes, add $\frac{1}{4}$ teaspoon citric acid to each 500 g (1 lb).

METHODS OF BOTTLING
The first two methods give a good appearance, but usually only a few bottles can be processed at a time. Using a pressure cooker saves time, but it is easy to overcook and shrink the fruit. Using the oven methods takes longer but more bottles can be processed together.

Method 1 – Slow heating in water

A thermometer is essential for this method. Pour in enough cold syrup to cover the fruit and almost fill the jars. Adjust clips or put screw bands on loosely. Use a pan deep enough for the jars to be completely immersed in cold water whilst standing on a base of wire, wood or cloth; they must not touch the bottom of the pan or they will crack. Separate them from each other with cloth. Cover with a lid or board.

Heat slowly so that after 1 hour the water temperature is only 54°C (130°F) and reaches the temperature given on the chart (see page 44) after a further 30 minutes. Maintain that temperature for the time given.

Ladle out enough water so the jars can be lifted out with a cloth or oven gloves. Put them on a wooden surface to prevent them cracking. Tighten screw bands at once; clips do not need attention.

Leave for 24 hours, then test for a seal (see opposite).

Method 2 – Quick heating in water

A thermometer is useful for this method. Proceed as for Method 1, but use warm jars and syrup or water at 60°C (140°F). Use warm water, 38°C (100°F) to fill the pan and

bring to simmering point, 88°C (190°F), in 25 or 30 minutes. Simmer for the time given on the chart (see page 45). Continue as for Method 1, testing for a seal (see below) after 24 hours.

Method 3 – Using a pressure cooker

Pour 2.5 cm (1 inch) water into the cooker, put in the rack and bring to the boil. Use warm jars and fill with boiling syrup or water to cover the fruit. Put on tops with clips, or screw bands loosened by a quarter turn. Put on the cooker lid but leave the vent open until steam starts to escape, then close. Bring to 2.25 kg (5 lb) pressure, then reduce the heat to keep at that temperature for the time given on the chart (see page 45). Remove the cooker from the heat, leave for 10 minutes then open. Continue as for Method 1, testing for a seal (see below) after 24 hours.

Method 4 – In a very cool oven

Preheat the oven to 120°C (250°F), Gas Mark $\frac{1}{2}$. Fill the jars with fruit and place on a baking sheet lined with 4 thicknesses of newspaper; do not add liquid or put on the lids. Put into the oven, leaving space for heat to circulate around the jars. Heat for the time given on the chart (see page 45), then remove them one at a time.

Fill the jars right to the top with boiling syrup or water. Put on the lids and seal. If the fruit has shrunk a great deal, use the fruit from one jar to fill up the others before adding the liquid.

Leave for 24 hours then test for a seal (see below).

Method 5 – In a cool oven

Preheat the oven to 150°C (300°F), Gas Mark 2. Fill the jars with boiling syrup or water to cover the fruit, put on the rubber rings and tops but not the clips or screwbands. Proceed as for Method 4. Remove from the oven one at a time and put on the clip or screwband at once.

Leave for 24 hours then test for a seal (see below).

Testing for a Seal

Leave the jars undisturbed for 24 hours. Remove the screw bands or clip tops and grip the lids only with the fingers of one hand. If the lid stays firm, a vacuum has been created; replace the screw bands or clip tops.

If the lid comes away, either use the fruit at once, or reprocess. Re-examine the jar for cracks or chips and change the rubber rings. Never process for a third time.

Storage

As long as the seal remains intact the fruit is safe to eat. It should, however, be used within about 3 years or the texture of the fruit may deteriorate.

Illustrated opposite: Bottling plums

Fruit	Sugar to 600 ml (1 pint) water	Method 1
Berries **Currants** **Gooseberries** } **Rhubarb**	375 g (12 oz) 500 g (1 lb) 250 g (8 oz)	74°C (165°F) maintain 10 minutes
Apple slices	to taste	74°C (165°F) maintain 10 minutes
Cherries – dark **Damsons** } **Plums – dark**	125 g (4 oz)	82°C (180°F) maintain 15 minutes
Apricots **Cherries – white** **Greengages** } **Plums – light**	250 g (8 oz) 125 g (4 oz)	82°C (180°F) maintain 15 minutes
Grapefruit **Lemons** } **Oranges**	125 g (4 oz)	82°C (180°F) maintain 15 minutes
Apple-pulp **Nectarines** } **Peaches**	to taste 250 g (8 oz)	82°C (180°F) maintain 15 minutes
Figs } **Pears** **Tomatoes – whole**	125 g (4 oz) —	88°C (190°F) maintain 30 minutes
Tomatoes **– solid pack**	—	88°C (190°F) maintain 40 minutes

Time is for 500 g–1 kg (1–2 lb) jars. For larger jars, allo

Method 2	Method 3	Method 4	Method 5
74°C (165°F) maintain 2 minutes	1 minute	45–55 minutes	30–40 minutes
74°C (165°F) maintain 2 minutes	1 minute	will discolour easily	30–40 minutes
82°C (180°F) maintain 10 minutes	1 minute	55–70 minutes	40–50 minutes
82°C (180°F) maintain 10 minutes	1 minute	will discolour easily	40–50 minutes
82°C (180°F) maintain 10 minutes	1 minute	not recommended	40–50 minutes
82°C (180°F) maintain 20 minutes	3–4 minutes	will discolour easily	50–60 minutes
88°C (190°F) maintain 40 minutes	5 minutes	will discolour easily	60–70 minutes
88°C (190°F) maintain 50 minutes	15 minutes	will discolour easily	70–80 minutes

extra 5 minutes (Methods 1 to 4), 10 minutes (Method 5).

PICKLES

Pickles, mainly vegetables and fruits, are preserved by salt and vinegar. Adding sugar or honey produces a more mellow pickle and adding spices gives additional flavour.

Salt: Used to extract moisture from some vegetables, which would otherwise dilute the vinegar and cause the pickle to ferment, and to toughen the vegetables.

Use dry salt for those with a high moisture content and a brine for a more gentle action. Use cooking salt rather than table salt; the latter contains iodine which can darken fruit.

Vinegar: Use bottled vinegars (malt, distilled, wine, cider, spiced, etc.); draught vinegars are not strong enough. Use cold vinegar for crisp pickles, boiling vinegar for softer ones. The vinegar should cover the pickle by 1–2.5 cm ($\frac{1}{2}$–1 inch).

For homemade spiced vinegar, boil 15–25 g ($\frac{1}{2}$–1 oz) mixed pickling spice in 600 ml (1 pint) vinegar for 5 minutes. Strain when cold.

Spices: Use whole spices; powdered ones will cloud the pickle. Mixed pickling spice is composed of equal quantities of stick cinnamon, allspice berries, cloves, mace and a few peppercorns. Root ginger, chillies, celery seeds, etc. can also be used.

Fruits: These are not salted or brined, but simmered until tender, usually in vinegar. They can also be simmered in syrup but this dilutes the vinegar when added; the vinegar is therefore boiled first to concentrate it.

Preparing Courgette and Onion Pickle

Vegetables: Some vegetables need to be cooked in water before pickling, others are cooked in the vinegar, and some do not need cooking: always follow the recipe.

Pans: Use unchipped enamel, aluminium or stainless steel pans. Copper, brass and iron ones react with vinegar and spoil the flavour.

Sealing: Jars must be sterilized (see page 5) and well sealed to prevent the vinegar evaporating and the contents drying. Metal lids corrode when in contact with vinegar and are therefore unsuitable. Glass or plastic-coated lids, corks previously soaked in boiling water for 15 minutes to sterilize, and Porosan skin are all satisfactory.

Paraffin wax can also be used; it is available from chemists. Melt the wax in a basin standing in a pan of hot water over a very low heat; do not let it get too hot or it may ignite. Wipe the inside of the neck of the jar with kitchen paper immediately after filling. Leave the pickle to cool to room temperature. Pour in 1 cm ($\frac{1}{2}$ inch) depth of wax and leave to set; if it shrinks a little on cooling, pour in a thin second layer. When the pickle is required, remove and wash the wax. It can be melted and re-used several times.

Maturing: Pickles should be allowed to mature before they are eaten. A minimum of 2 to 4 weeks maturing is usually recommended. Crisp pickles tend to soften after about 3 months.

Crunchy Pickled Celery

500 g (1 lb) celery
4 onions
2 green peppers,
  cored and seeded
2 red peppers, cored
  and seeded
250 g (8 oz) sugar
4 teaspoons salt
4 teaspoons mustard
  seeds
1 teaspoon ground
  turmeric
600 ml (1 pint)
  distilled white malt
  vinegar
2 tablespoons corn-
  flour blended with
  3 tablespoons water

Slice the celery, onions and green
peppers thinly; dice the red peppers.
Put the vegetables in a bowl and
cover with boiling water. Leave to
stand for 10 minutes, then drain.

Meanwhile, put the sugar, salt,
mustard seeds, turmeric and vinegar in
a pan. Bring to the boil, add the
vegetables and boil, stirring, for
5 minutes. Add the blended cornflour
and boil for a further 3 minutes.

Pour into hot sterilized jars and seal.

This is excellent with fish dishes and
cold meats.

Makes about 1.5 kg (3 lb)

Red Cabbage and Onion Pickle

750 g (1½ lb) red
   cabbage
250 g (8 oz) pickling
   onions
65 g (2½ oz) salt
450 ml (¾ pint) red
   wine vinegar
50 g (2 oz) sugar
150 ml (¼ pint) water
1 cinnamon stick,
   broken
4 cloves
¼ teaspoon allspice
   berries
1 large piece root
   ginger, roughly
   chopped
6 black peppercorns

Cut the cabbage into quarters and
remove the core. Wash well then cut
across into 1 cm (½ inch) shreds. Put
into a basin with the onions and salt.
Mix well and leave to stand for
24 hours, stirring several times. Rinse
quickly under cold running water;
drain thoroughly. Pack into hot
sterilized jars.

   Put the vinegar, sugar and water in a
pan. Place the spices on a small square
of muslin and tie firmly; add to the
pan. Bring to the boil and simmer for
15 minutes. Remove the muslin bag.
Pour the boiling vinegar over the
cabbage, removing any air bubbles in
the jars with a skewer. Seal.

   Serve with frankfurters and other
sausages.

Makes about 1.5 kg (3 lb)

Pickled Cucumbers with Dill

500 g (1 lb) cucumbers
   7.5–10 cm
   (3–4 inches) long
2 heads fresh dill
2 cloves garlic,
   halved
40 g (1½ oz) salt
300 ml (½ pint) white
   wine vinegar
450 ml (¾ pint) water
4 black peppercorns

Scrub the cucumbers and trim the ends. Cover with iced water and leave to soak for 24 hours. Drain and prick all over with a skewer. Put 1 head of dill and the garlic into a large hot sterilized jar. Pack in the cucumbers and put the other head of dill on top.

Place the salt, vinegar, water and peppercorns in a pan and bring to the boil. Pour over the cucumbers and seal.

Serve with ham and other boiled meats.

Makes about 1.5 kg (3 lb)

Beetroot and Horseradish Pickle

1 kg (2 lb) small
   beetroot, cooked and
   diced
50 g (2 oz)
   horseradish, grated
50 g (2 oz) sugar
600 ml (1 pint) red
   wine vinegar
1 teaspoon salt
1 teaspoon pickling
   spice, tied in
   muslin

Mix the beetroot and horseradish together and pack into hot sterilized jars.

Put the sugar, vinegar, salt and muslin bag in a pan, bring to the boil and simmer for 15 minutes. Remove the muslin bag. Pour the boiling vinegar over the beetroot and seal.

Makes about 1.25 kg (2½ lb)

Courgette and Onion Pickle

500 g (1 lb) small
   courgettes
450 ml (¾ pint) white
   wine vinegar
25 g (1 oz) sugar
1½ teaspoons salt
1½ teaspoons black
   peppercorns
2 tablespoons cold
   water
125 g (4 oz) small
   pickling onions

Cut the courgettes in half lengthways, then into quarters. Put the vinegar, sugar, salt, peppercorns and water in a pan, bring to the boil and simmer for 5 minutes. Add the courgettes and onions and bring back to simmering point, stirring.

Pack the vegetables into hot sterilized jars and cover with the vinegar. Seal.

Serve with lamb dishes.

Makes about 750 g (1½ lb)

Garlic Pickled Peppers

6 long, thin peppers,
    weighing about
    500 g (1 lb)
2 tablespoons salt
¼ teaspoon ground
    allspice
¼ teaspoon celery
    seeds
½ teaspoon mustard
    seeds
3 cloves garlic,
    thinly sliced
900 ml (1½ pints)
    Garlic vinegar
    (see page 82)
1 tablespoon
    granulated sugar
8 black peppercorns

Cut the tops off the peppers and scoop out the seeds and core. Place the whole peppers in a basin, sprinkle with the salt and cover with boiling water. Leave to stand for 2 hours, then drain well.

Mix the allspice with the celery and mustard seeds and sprinkle a little into each of the peppers. Pack into hot sterilized jars and add the garlic.

Place the vinegar, sugar and peppercorns in a pan and bring to the boil. Pour over the peppers and seal.

Serve as an accompaniment to mild curries and cold meats.

Makes about 1.5 kg (3 lb)

Pickled Mushrooms

2 litres (3½ pints)
    water
6 teaspoons salt
1.5 kg (3 lb) button
    mushrooms
2 onions, diced
900 ml (1½ pints)
    Tarragon vinegar
    (see page 82)
2 tablespoons
    pickling spice
2 cloves garlic, sliced
2 bay leaves
2 tablespoons juniper
    berries

Place 1.75 litres (3 pints) of the water
and 2 teaspoons of the salt in a pan
and bring to the boil. Add the mushrooms and simmer for 1 hour. Drain
and rinse in iced water.

Meanwhile, sprinkle the onion with
2 teaspoons of the salt and leave to
stand for 20 minutes. Rinse and drain
thoroughly.

Put the remaining water and salt in
a pan with the vinegar. Place the
pickling spice, garlic and bay leaves on
a small square of muslin and tie firmly;
add to the pan. Bring to the boil and
boil for 10 minutes. Add the mushrooms and bring back to the boil.
Remove the muslin bag.

Pack the mushrooms into hot
sterilized jars, sprinkling the onion and
the juniper berries between the layers.
Cover with the hot vinegar and seal.

Serve as part of a mixed hors
d'oeuvres or with grilled meats.

Makes about 1.5 kg (3½ lb)

Spiced Green Beans

300 ml (½ pint) cold water
1½ teaspoons salt
500 g (1 lb) small French beans, trimmed
1 tablespoon pickling spice
4 strips lemon rind
25 g (1 oz) sugar
450 ml (¾ pint) cider vinegar
150 ml (¼ pint) hot water

Put the cold water and salt in a pan, bring to the boil and add the beans. Cover and simmer for 10 minutes; drain.

Place the pickling spice and lemon rind on a small square of muslin and tie firmly. Place in a pan with the remaining ingredients, bring to the boil and boil for 5 minutes. Add the beans and simmer for a further 5 minutes. Pack the beans into hot sterilized jars. Remove the muslin bag from the vinegar, pour over the beans and seal.

Serve with salads.

Makes about 1.25 kg (2½ lb)

Piccallili

500 g (1 lb) marrow
125 g (4 oz) runner beans
1 small cauliflower, broken into florets
500 g (1 lb) pickling onions
250 g (8 oz) cooking apples
175 g (6 oz) salt
1.75 litres (3 pints) water (optional)
3 fresh chillies, red or green
3 cloves
25 g (1 oz) root ginger, crushed
900 ml (1½ pints) plus 2 tablespoons distilled white malt vinegar
125 g (4 oz) sugar
25 g (1 oz) mustard powder
1 tablespoon turmeric
1 tablespoon cornflour

Cut the vegetables and apples into 1–2.5 cm (½–1 inch) pieces. Place on a large dish, sprinkle with the salt and leave to stand overnight.

Alternatively, dissolve the salt in the water, add the vegetables, cover with a plate to keep them submerged and leave to stand for 48 hours. Rinse and dry the vegetables.

Put the chillies, cloves and ginger on a small square of muslin and tie firmly. Place in a pan with 900 ml (1½ pints) of the vinegar and simmer for 20 minutes. Remove the muslin bag. Add the vegetables and sugar to the pan and simmer for a further 20 minutes.

Mix the mustard powder, turmeric and cornflour to a smooth paste with the remaining vinegar. Add to the pan and bring to the boil, stirring; boil for 3 minutes, stirring constantly. Pour into hot sterilized jars and seal.

Makes about 2.5 kg (5½ lb)

Pickled Eggs

300 ml (½ pint)
   Tarragon vinegar
   (see page 82)
150 ml (¼ pint) water
1 clove garlic, crushed
1 teaspoon pickling
   spice
1 tablespoon sugar
2 dried red chillies
6 hard-boiled eggs,
   shelled

Put all the ingredients, except the eggs, in a pan, bring to the boil and simmer for 15 minutes. Leave until cold, then strain. Place the eggs in a glass jar, cover with the vinegar and seal.

   Use within 4 weeks.

Makes 6

Pickled Walnuts

Walnuts for pickling are available from late June.

BRINE:
2.25 litres (4 pints)
   boiling water
500 g (1 lb) salt
PICKLE:
1 kg (2 lb) green
   walnuts
1.2 litres (2 pints)
   distilled white
   malt vinegar
25 g (1 oz) black
   peppercorns
1 large piece root
   ginger, roughly
   chopped
1 blade mace
1 teaspoon allspice
   berries
1 tablespoon salt

Make the brine by pouring 1.2 litres (2 pints) boiling water onto 250 g (8 oz) of the salt. Stir until dissolved, then leave until cold.

   Prick each walnut with a skewer, discarding any in which the beginnings of a hard shell can be felt. Put them in a bowl, pour in the cold brine and weigh down with a plate to make sure they remain submerged. Leave for 6 days.

   Make another brine mixture from the remaining water and salt. Drain off the first brine and replace with the fresh brine. Leave for a further 6 days.

   Drain and spread out the walnuts, in a single layer, on a large dish. Leave in a warm place, in sunshine if possible, until they turn black; this should take 1 to 2 days. Pack into sterilized jars.

   Place the remaining ingredients in a pan, bring to the boil and simmer for 10 minutes. Leave until cold. Strain, pour over the walnuts and seal.

   These are good with all cold meats.

Makes about 1.5 kg (3 lb)

NOTE: For a sweeter pickle, dissolve up to 750 g (1½ lb) soft dark brown sugar in the vinegar before it boils.

Pickled Prunes

1 lemon
350 g (12 oz) prunes
350 ml (12 fl oz) red
  wine vinegar
175 g (6 oz) sugar
1 tablespoon pickling
  spice
1 small piece
  cinnamon stick

Squeeze the juice from the lemon and make up to 600 ml (1 pint) with water; keep the rind. Put the prunes in a basin, pour over the lemon juice and leave for 24 hours. Transfer to a pan and simmer for about 15 minutes, until tender. Drain, reserving the liquid.

Pare the rind from the lemon halves and put into a pan with the vinegar, sugar and spices. Bring to the boil, simmer for 10 minutes, then strain. Add 150 ml (¼ pint) of the reserved liquid and the prunes and bring back to the boil.

Pack the prunes into hot sterilized jars, cover with the vinegar and seal.

Serve with hot or cold pork.

Makes about 750 g (1½ lb)

Sweet and Sour Melon Pickle

1 × 1.75 kg (4 lb)
  barely ripe, yellow
  or green honeydew
  melon
2 tablespoons salt
1 teaspoon pickling
  spice
1 small piece root
  ginger, chopped
300 ml (½ pint) white
  wine vinegar
750 g (1½ lb)
  granulated sugar

Cut the melon into quarters and discard the seeds and skin. Cut into strips and put in a colander. Sprinkle with the salt and leave to stand for 2 hours. Pour boiling water over the melon to remove all the salt.

Place the spices on a small square of muslin and tie firmly.

Put the melon in a pan with the vinegar and muslin bag. Bring slowly to the boil and simmer for 5 minutes. Remove from the heat and leave for about 1 hour or until cold.

Add the sugar to the pan and heat slowly, stirring, until dissolved, then bring to the boil and simmer for 5 minutes.

Pack the melon into hot sterilized jars. Bring the liquid back to the boil and remove the muslin bag. Pour over the melon and seal.

This pickle is delicious with prawns or shrimps served in their shells. It is also very good served with salads.

Makes about 1.5 kg (3 lb)

Pickled Grapes

350 g (12 oz) seedless
  white grapes
350 g (12 oz) black
  grapes, seeded
75 g (3 oz) sugar
2 teaspoons salt
300 ml ($\frac{1}{2}$ pint)
  cider vinegar
250 ml (8 fl oz) water
1 tablespoon white
  peppercorns

Pack the grapes into sterilized jars.
Place the remaining ingredients in a
basin and stir until the sugar and the
salt are dissolved, then chill. Pour over
the grapes and seal.

These are especially good with
grilled or baked white fish.

Makes about 1.5 kg (3 lb)

CHUTNEYS & RELISHES

These are usually served as accompaniments to hot and cold foods. They can also be used to add flavour to scrambled eggs, stuffings, sandwich fillings, cottage cheese and savoury dips. They can also be added to stews and casseroles before cooking; sauces, marinades and glazes; cooked rice for savoury dishes, and to all types of salad dressings.

CHUTNEYS
Vegetables and fruits are cooked with salt, spices, sugar and vinegar until they are soft and smooth in texture.

Ingredients: Cut, chop or mince basic ingredients so that they soften more quickly. To provide a contrast in textures, add small amounts of dried fruits, nuts, crystallized ginger, etc. Whole spices, tied in muslin and removed before bottling, or ground spices can be used. Cooking salt and bottled vinegars should be used as for pickles (see page 46).

Cooking: Long slow cooking is necessary to produce a soft mixture with a mature flavour and dark colour. A lighter chutney can be made if the sugar is added towards the end of cooking time, when the mixture thickens.

Equipment: Use the pans recommended for pickles (see page 47). If the chutney is to be sieved, use a nylon or hair sieve. Always use hot sterilized jars (see page 5) and vinegar-proof airtight covers (see page 47).

RELISHES
These are 'mid-way' between pickles and chutneys. They can be sweet or sour, spiced or plain.

Cut the fruits and vegetables into pieces, about the size of corn kernels. Cooking time is shorter than for chutneys so ingredients retain their shape. Use the same equipment and seals as for pickles (see page 46–7). Use small jars.

Banana Chutney

2 onions, chopped
12 very firm bananas
a little lemon juice
300 ml (½ pint)
   distilled white
   malt vinegar
125 g (4 oz) sultanas
2 teaspoons curry
   powder
250 g (8 oz) sugar
1 teaspoon salt

Cook the onions in water to cover for 5 minutes to soften; drain. Slice the bananas and toss in lemon juice. Put the onions, bananas, vinegar, sultanas and curry powder in a pan. Bring to the boil and simmer until thick.

Add the sugar and salt, stirring until dissolved. Cook gently until the chutney thickens again.

Pour into hot sterilized jars and seal.
Makes about 1.5 kg (3 lb)

Apricot and Date Chutney

500 g (1 lb) dried
    apricots
275 g (9 oz) sultanas
350 ml (12 fl oz)
    white wine vinegar
125 g (4 oz) soft
    dark brown sugar
250 g (8 oz) fresh dates
125 g (4 oz) preserved
    stem ginger,
    chopped
250 ml (8 fl oz) water
1 tablespoon salt
1½ teaspoons mustard
    seeds
½ teaspoon chilli
    powder

Cover the apricots with water and
leave to soak for 1 hour; drain. Place
in a pan with the sultanas and vinegar,
bring slowly to the boil and simmer for
15 minutes.

Stir in the remaining ingredients and
simmer until thickened.

Pour into hot sterilized jars and seal.

Makes about 1 kg (2 lb)

Apple and Mint Chutney

1.5 kg (3 lb) cooking
  apples, peeled, cored
  and chopped
900 ml (1½ pints)
  spiced vinegar
  (see page 46)
½ teaspoon coriander
  seeds
1 teaspoon black
  peppercorns,
  crushed
2 dried red chillies
500 g (1 lb) demerara
  sugar
2 teaspoons salt
2 tablespoons chopped
  mint

Put the apples in a pan with the vinegar
and bring slowly to boiling point.
Place the spices and chillies on a square
of muslin and tie firmly. Add to the
pan with the sugar and salt. Simmer
until thickened. Remove the muslin
bag and stir in the mint.

Pour into hot sterilized jars and seal.
Makes about 1.5 kg (3 lb)

Cucumber and Cherry Chutney

750 g (1½ lb)
  cucumbers
3 onions
500 g (1 lb) red
  cherries
450 ml (¾ pint) red
  wine vinegar
250 g (8 oz) sugar
1 tablespoon salt
1 teaspoon ground
  ginger
1 teaspoon cumin
  seeds
2 tablespoons
  arrowroot blended
  with 4 tablespoons
  cold water

Cut the cucumbers in half lengthways
and scoop out the seeds. Slice as finely
as possible. Cut the onions into
quarters, then into very thin slices.
Halve or quarter the cherries, discarding
the stones.

Put the cucumber, onion and cherries
in a pan with the vinegar, sugar, salt
and spices. Heat gently, stirring, until
the sugar has dissolved, then bring to
the boil and simmer for 20 to 30
minutes, until the cucumber is very soft.

Stir in the blended arrowroot and
simmer for a further 5 minutes. Pour
into hot sterilized jars and seal.

Makes about 1.75 kg (4 lb)

Rhubarb and Fresh Ginger Chutney

350 g (12 oz) dessert
  apples, peeled and
  cored
350 g (12 oz) onions
25 g (1 oz) fresh root
  ginger, peeled
2 cloves garlic
1.5 kg (3 lb) rhubarb,
  thinly sliced
2 teaspoons paprika
15 g (½ oz) salt
450 ml (¾ pint) red
  wine vinegar
juice of 1 orange
1 tablespoon tomato
  purée
750 g (1½ lb) sugar

Mince the apples, onions, ginger and garlic. Place in a pan with the rhubarb, paprika, salt, vinegar, orange juice and tomato purée. Stir well, bring to the boil and simmer until pulpy.

When the mixture is very thick, add the sugar and stir until dissolved. Bring back to the boil and boil rapidly until the chutney thickens.

Pour into hot, sterilized jars and seal.
Makes about 2.25 kg (5 lb)

Green Tomato Chutney

2.25 kg (5 lb) green
  tomatoes
500 g (1 lb) onions
25 g (1 oz) salt
250 g (8 oz) seedless
  raisins
250 g (8 oz) sultanas
1 tablespoon whole
  black peppercorns
15 g (½ oz) root
  ginger, roughly
  chopped
1 tablespoon coriander
  seeds
12 cloves
4 dried red chillies
500 g (1 lb) demerara
  sugar
1.2 litres (2 pints)
  Garlic vinegar
  (see page 82)

Cut up or slice the tomatoes and onions. Place in a bowl, sprinkle with the salt and leave overnight; drain.

Place in a pan with the raisins and sultanas. Place the spices and chillies on a square of muslin and tie firmly; add to the pan with the sugar and vinegar. Simmer until thickened, stirring frequently. Remove the muslin bag.

Pour into hot sterilized jars and seal.
Makes about 2.25 kg (5 lb)

Hot Aubergine Chutney

1 kg (2 lb) aubergines,
  sliced
3 tablespoons salt
175 g (6 oz) soft
  dark brown sugar
350 ml (12 fl oz)
  white wine vinegar
75 g (3 oz) raisins,
  stoned
1 tablespoon tomato
  purée
5 cloves garlic,
  crushed
4 celery sticks,
  finely chopped
250 g (8 oz) onions,
  finely chopped
1 teaspoon cayenne
  pepper
2 dried red chillies,
  chopped

Put the aubergines in a colander and
sprinkle with the salt. Leave for about
4 hours, then rinse and dry.

Put the sugar, vinegar, raisins and
tomato purée in a basin and leave to
soak for 4 hours.

Place all the ingredients in a pan
and heat gently, stirring until the
sugar is dissolved, then simmer until
thickened. Pour into hot sterilized jars
and seal.

Makes about 1.5 kg (3 lb)

Courgette Chutney

750 g (1½ lb)
  courgettes, sliced
1½ tablespoons salt
250 g (8 oz) ripe
  tomatoes, skinned
  and chopped
125 g (4 oz) onions,
  chopped
125 g (4 oz) sultanas
1 tablespoon coarsely
  grated orange rind
500 g (1 lb) sugar
350 ml (12 fl oz)
  spiced vinegar
  (see page 46)
1 teaspoon ground
  cinnamon
50 g (2 oz) walnuts,
  chopped

Put the courgettes in a colander and
sprinkle with the salt. Leave for
2 hours, then rinse and dry.

Put in a pan with the remaining
ingredients, except the walnuts, and
heat gently, stirring, until the sugar
has dissolved. Simmer until thickened,
then stir in the walnuts.

Pour into hot sterilized jars and seal.

Makes about 1.5 kg (3 lb)

Curry Relish

250 g (8 oz) aubergines
175 g (6 oz) onion
250 g (8 oz) carrot
125 g (4 oz) sweetcorn
125 g (4 oz) peas
250 g (8 oz) tiny
  cauliflower florets
1½ tablespoons salt
450 ml (¾ pint) cider
  vinegar
150 ml (¼ pint) water
175 g (6 oz) soft
  dark brown sugar
1 teaspoon coriander
  seeds
½ teaspoon ground
  ginger
15 g (½ oz) pickling
  spice, tied in muslin
1½ teaspoons curry
  powder
25 g (1 oz) flaked
  almonds
1 tablespoon cornflour
2 tablespoons water

Cut the aubergines in half lengthways, then across into very thin slices. Grate the onion and carrot. Put into a bowl with the remaining vegetables and the salt. Pour in enough water just to cover and leave to stand overnight.

Drain well and squeeze with the hands to extract as much water as possible.

Put the remaining ingredients, except the almonds, cornflour and water, in a pan, bring to the boil and simmer for 20 minutes.

Add the vegetables and nuts, cover and simmer for 10 minutes. Remove the lid and boil fast for 7 minutes. Remove the muslin bag.

Blend the cornflour and water together and stir into the pan. Boil for 3 minutes.

Pour into hot sterilized jars and seal.
Makes about 1.5 kg (3 lb)

Cucumber and Red Pepper Relish

750 g (1½ lb) medium
  cucumbers, peeled
2 teaspoons salt
2 large red peppers,
  cored, seeded and
  thinly sliced
1 tablespoon lime
  juice
175 ml (6 fl oz) red
  wine vinegar
2 teaspoons mustard
  seeds

Cut the cucumbers in half lengthways
and remove the seeds. Mince coarsely
into a colander or sieve, sprinkle with
the salt and leave for at least 1 hour.
Squeeze out excess moisture.

Put the peppers and lime juice in a
bowl and mix well.

Bring the vinegar to the boil and add
the cucumber, peppers, any remaining
lime juice, and mustard seeds. Simmer
for 10 minutes.

Pour into hot sterilized jars and seal.

Makes about 750 g (1¾ lb)

Pineapple Relish

2 × 439 g (15½ oz)
  cans pineapple pieces
2 fresh red chillies
2 fresh green chillies
250 g (8 oz) onions
15 g (½ oz) root
  ginger, chopped
1 blade mace
1 tablespoon whole
  grain mustard
2 teaspoons salt
300 ml (½ pint) Garlic
  vinegar (see page 82)

Drain the pineapple, reserving the juice. Mince coarsely with the chillies and onions. Put the spices on a square of muslin and tie firmly. Blend the mustard with 300 ml (½ pint) of the pineapple juice.

Put all the ingredients in a pan and boil gently, stirring occasionally, until the onion is cooked and there is just enough liquid to stop the mixture sticking to the pan. Pour into hot sterilized jars and seal.

Makes about 750 (1½ lb)

Cranberry Relish

1 large orange
500 g (1 lb)
  cranberries
250 g (8 oz) sugar
2 firm pears, peeled,
  cored and diced
200 ml (⅓ pint) red
  wine vinegar
2 teaspoons salt

Pare the rind from the orange in long pieces, then cut across into fine strips. Place in a pan with the cranberries, sugar and pears.

Squeeze the juice from the orange and make up to 300 ml (½ pint) with the vinegar. Add to the pan with the salt. Heat gently, stirring until the sugar is dissolved, then simmer for 10 to 15 minutes until the fruit is just tender. Pour into hot sterilized jars; seal.

Makes about 750 g (1½ lb)

Lemon Relish

2 large lemons
1 red or green pepper
6 large spring onions
2 large celery sticks
1 fresh red chilli
4 parsley sprigs
½ teaspoon dry mustard
½ teaspoon ground
  cardamon
1 teaspoon salt
2 tablespoons sugar
120 ml (4 fl oz) Chilli
  vinegar (see page 82)

Pare the rind from the lemons. Cut off and discard the white pith. Remove the core and seeds from the pepper.

Coarsely mince the lemon rind and flesh, onions (including the green tops), pepper, celery, chilli and parsley. Put into a pan with the remaining ingredients, bring to the boil and simmer for 15 minutes. Pour into hot sterilized jars and seal.

Makes about 500 g (1 lb)

SAUCES & KETCHUPS, OILS & VINEGARS

SAUCES AND KETCHUPS

These are made in much the same way as chutneys, using similar ingredients, cooking salt and bottled vinegars. Use the same type of pans and seals as for pickles (see page 47) and hot sterilized jars (see page 5).

Those made from ripe tomatoes and mushrooms may ferment unless they are sterilized immediately after bottling. Follow the instructions for the hot method of sterilizing fruit syrups and squashes (see page 84). Sauces are rubbed through a nylon or hair sieve after cooking to give a smooth mixture, then cooked again until they are thick enough not to separate out on standing, but will still pour; they thicken as they cool. Metal sieves and electric blenders with metal blades should not be used to purée the sauces, because contact with metal tends to reduce their keeping qualities. Ketchups are strained through a nylon jelly bag and are not as thick.

OILS AND VINEGARS

These are generally flavoured with herbs, but strongly flavoured ingredients such as chillies, garlic, lemon and orange rind can also be used, or a combination of flavours.

Preparing Fruit sauce

Fruits, usually soft fruits such as raspberries, strawberries and blackberries, can also be used to flavour vinegars.

The recipes chosen give the basic instructions; follow them, adapting to use flavourings of your choice.

Flavoured oils: Add interest to mayonnaise and salad dressings. They can also be used to give subtle flavours to casseroles by sealing the meat in an appropriate oil, e.g. sage for pork, rosemary for lamb; to roasts and grills by brushing the meat with an oil before cooking; and to sauces by using them instead of other fats.

Flavoured vinegars: These can be used in pickles, chutneys and sauces. Herb-flavoured vinegars make delicious salad dressings and mayonnaise. Small quantities can be added to savoury sauces, casseroles, curries, fish dishes, etc. They can also be used to add unexpected flavours to pickles, chutneys and sauces. Fruit-flavoured vinegars make refreshing drinks when diluted with iced water or soda water. Small quantities can also be added to sweet sauces.

Storage: Both oils and vinegars tend to lose their flavour after about 4 months.

Chilli Sauce

175 g (6 oz) fresh
chillies, red, green
and yellow
175 g (6 oz) onion,
finely chopped
125 g (4 oz) cooking
apple, peeled, cored
and chopped
2 teaspoons prepared
mustard
1 teaspoon salt
150 ml ($\frac{1}{4}$ pint)
distilled white malt
vinegar

Wearing rubber gloves and taking care not to touch the eyes, remove the stalks and seeds from the chillies and chop as finely as possible. Put in a pan with the remaining ingredients. Heat gently, stirring, until the mixture boils, then simmer until all the ingredients are soft and mushy and the sauce has thickened, about 40 minutes. Sieve, pour immediately into a hot sterilized bottle and seal.

Makes about 450 ml ($\frac{3}{4}$ pint)

NOTE: This sauce tends to separate on standing, so shake the bottle before use.

Tomato and Pepper Sauce

1.5 kg (3 lb) large,
  ripe tomatoes
350 g (12 oz) large
  green peppers, cored
  and seeded
500 g (1 lb) large
  onions
2 teaspoons salt
½ teaspoon mustard
  seeds
½ teaspoon ground
  allspice
½ teaspoon ground
  cloves
450 ml (¾ pint) Chilli
  vinegar (see
  page 82)
125 g (4 oz) sugar

Mince or chop the vegetables. Put in
a pan with the salt, flavourings and
vinegar. Bring slowly to the boil and
simmer for about 30 minutes or until
the vegetables are very soft, then sieve.

Return to the pan, add the sugar and
heat gently, stirring, until dissolved.
Simmer for about 1 hour or until the
sauce is very thick. Pour into a hot
sterilized bottle and sterilize (see
page 72).

Makes about 600 ml (1 pint)

Spicy Tomato Sauce

1.5 kg (3 lb) ripe
  tomatoes, chopped
250 g (8 oz) onions,
  chopped
2 teaspoons salt
2 cloves
10 black peppercorns,
  crushed
1 bay leaf
300 ml (½ pint)
  spiced vinegar
  (see page 46)
75 g (3 oz) sugar
1 teaspoon cayenne
  pepper
2 teaspoons paprika
2–3 teaspoons chilli
  powder

Put the tomatoes, onions, salt, cloves, peppercorns, bay leaf and vinegar in a pan and simmer for about 1 hour until cooked and well blended. Sieve, return to the pan and boil rapidly until thickened.

Add the remaining ingredients and stir until the sugar has dissolved.

Pour into a hot sterilized bottle and sterilize (see page 72).

Makes 450–600 ml ($\frac{3}{4}$–1 pint)

Plum Sauce

1 kg (2 lb) bright red
  plums, stoned and
  chopped
175 g (6 oz) onions,
  sliced
2 fresh red chillies,
  seeded and chopped
1 tablespoon salt
600 ml (1 pint)
  spiced vinegar
  (see page 46)
1 teaspoon allspice
  berries
1 small piece root
  ginger, roughly
  chopped
125 g (4 oz) sugar
1 teaspoon ground
  cinnamon or ground
  mace

Put the plums, onion, chillies, salt and half the vinegar in a pan. Place the allspice berries and root ginger on a square of muslin, tie together firmly and add to the pan. Simmer for 30 minutes, or until the fruit is soft and broken down. Remove the muslin bag.

Sieve and return to the pan. Add the remaining ingredients and stir until the sugar has dissolved. Simmer until thickened; this may take up to 1 hour. Pour into hot sterilized bottles and seal.

Makes about 900 ml (1$\frac{1}{2}$ pints)

Fruit Sauce

500 g (1 lb) cooking
apples
1 kg (2 lb) ripe
tomatoes
500 g (1 lb) firm
cooking pears
125 g (4 oz) currants
350 g (12 oz) onion,
chopped
2 teaspoons salt
$\frac{1}{4}$ teaspoon cayenne
pepper
2 teaspoons mustard
powder
300 ml ($\frac{1}{2}$ pint)
distilled white malt
vinegar

Cut up the apples, tomatoes and pears, without peeling. Put in a pan with the currants and onion. Simmer until all the ingredients are very soft; this may take up to 2 hours if the pears are very hard.

Sieve and return to the pan. Mix the remaining ingredients together and add to the pan. Bring to the boil and boil for 3 minutes, or until the sauce is thick.

Pour into hot sterilized bottles and sterilize (see page 72).

Makes about 1.2 litres (2 pints)

Gooseberry Ketchup

1 kg (2 lb) slightly
    under-ripe
    gooseberries
3 cloves garlic
1 tablespoon salt
1 teaspoon cayenne
    pepper
1 tablespoon mustard
    seeds
900 ml (1½ pints)
    white wine vinegar
350 g (12 oz)
    demerara sugar
125 g (4 oz) sultanas

Mince the gooseberries and garlic
together. Put in a pan with the
remaining ingredients. Cover and
simmer for 30 minutes, or until the
fruit is very soft and has really
flavoured the vinegar. Strain, pour into
hot sterilized bottles and seal.

Makes about 1 litre (1¾ pints)

Mushroom Ketchup

Use large, open mushrooms for this. Trim off the ends of the stalks and wipe with a slightly damp cloth. *Do not* wash or peel them.

1 kg (2 lb) large,
  open mushrooms,
  chopped
50 g (2 oz) salt
15 g ($\frac{1}{2}$ oz) ground
  allspice
1 small piece root
  ginger, roughly
  chopped
2 mace blades
1 shallot, finely
  chopped
600 ml (1 pint) red
  wine vinegar

Layer the mushrooms and salt in a lidded jar. Cover and leave for 2 days, stirring 4 times.

Place in a pan with the remaining ingredients. Cover and simmer for 30 minutes. Strain and pour into hot sterilized bottles.

Sterilize by the hot method for 30 minutes (see page 72).

Makes about 1.2 litres (2 pints)

Garlic and Chilli Oil

4 fresh red chillies
4 large cloves garlic,
    halved
600 ml (1 pint) good
    quality oil

Wearing rubber gloves and taking care not to touch the eyes, trim the chillies, split open and remove the seeds. Put into a jar with the garlic. Heat the oil very carefully until it is just a little warmer than blood heat; test with a finger. Pour into the jar and cover tightly.

Leave to stand in a sunny window for 1 to 2 weeks. Strain through 2 thicknesses of muslin. Pour into a sterilized bottle (see page 5) and seal with a sterilized cork or screw-top (see page 84).

Makes about 600 ml (1 pint)

NOTE: Warming the oil before adding to the flavouring speeds the infusion.

Salad Cream

175 ml (6 fl oz) milk
120 ml (4 fl oz)
    white wine vinegar
2 tablespoons sugar
1 tablespoon French
    mustard
125 g (4 oz) butter
4 medium eggs
¼ teaspoon salt
freshly ground white
    pepper

Put all the ingredients, with pepper to taste, in a pan and whisk together until blended. Heat gently, whisking all the time, until the mixture thickens. Pour into a hot sterilized bottle and seal.

Makes 450 ml ($\frac{3}{4}$ pint)

Variations

Add tomato purée, anchovy sauce, curry powder, chopped hard-boiled eggs, etc., or any flavouring of your choice.

Add chopped herbs which complement the food with which it is served, e.g. tarragon with chicken, basil with pasta salad.

Add chopped capers, gherkins, parsley, tarragon and chervil to make a tartare cream to serve with grilled meats and fish.

Rosemary Oil

6 good rosemary
   sprigs
600 ml (1 pint)
   good quality oil

Put the rosemary in a bottle, pour in the oil and cover tightly. Leave to stand in a sunny window for 2 to 4 weeks.

Strain through 2 thicknesses of muslin. Pour into a sterilized bottle (see page 5) and seal with a sterilized cork or screw-top (see page 84).

Makes about 600 ml (1 pint)

NOTE: This cold oil method is the best one to use with green herbs.

Tarragon Vinegar

2–3 good handfuls
  fresh tarragon
  leaves, roughly
  chopped
600 ml (1 pint) white
  wine vinegar or
  distilled white
  malt vinegar

Put the tarragon into a wide-mouthed
jar and pour over the vinegar. Cover
tightly and leave to stand, preferably
in a sunny window, for 2 to 4 weeks.
  Strain through muslin, pour into a
sterilized bottle (see page 5) and seal
as for pickles (see page 47).

Makes about 600 ml (1 pint)

Garlic vinegar: Prepare as above,
using 8–9 cloves garlic instead of
tarragon. Bring vinegar to the boil
before pouring over the garlic.

Chilli vinegar: Prepare as above,
using 20–25 chillies in place of the
tarragon. Bring vinegar to the boil,
add chillies and return to the boil,
before bottling. Leave to stand for
5 to 6 weeks before straining.

Raspberry Vinegar

1 kg (2 lb) raspberries
600 ml (1 pint)
  distilled white
  malt vinegar
sugar (see below)

Crush the raspberries with a wooden
spoon and put into a jar with the
vinegar. Cover and leave to stand for
7 days, stirring several times a day.
Strain through a jelly bag, squeezing
out as much juice as possible.
  Measure the juice and add 125–500 g
(4 oz–1 lb) sugar to each pint. Put in a
pan and heat gently, stirring, until the
sugar has dissolved, then boil rapidly
for 10 minutes.
  Pour into hot sterilized bottles (see
page 5) and seal as for pickles (see page
47).

Makes about 900 ml (1½ pints)

NOTE: The amount of sugar used
depends on personal taste. It is better
to under-sweeten as more can be
added when serving.

FRUIT SYRUPS, SQUASHES & LIQUEURS

SYRUPS AND SQUASHES

Syrups are strained fruit juices sweetened with sugar, whilst squashes have part of the fruit tissue included. Citrus fruits are mainly made into squashes and other fruits into syrups. Both can be diluted with water or soda for refreshing drinks; syrups can also be diluted with milk to make milk shakes, and used in a concentrated form as sauces to serve with ices, sponge puddings and fruit. Fuit must be in good condition, but fruit too ripe for bottling or jam-making is ideal.

Fermentation: Fruits rich in pectin are fermented to break down the pectin and prevent the syrup forming a jelly. This will take up to 5 days. If fermentation is allowed to continue for too long the flavour of the syrup will be affected.

Bottles: Use hot sterilized bottles (see page 5). Those with screw-tops should be filled to within 2.5 cm (1 inch) of the top and those with corks to within 3.5 cm (1½ inches). Corks must be new. Sterilize corks and screw-tops by covering with boiling water and leaving to stand for 15 minutes before using.

Sterilizing: Syrups and squashes *must* be sterilized or they will ferment. This can be done in two ways:

Hot method: Stand the filled bottles in a deep pan as for Method 1 – Fruit bottling (see page 42). Either keep at 77°C (170°F) for 30 minutes, or at simmering point, 88°C (190°F), for 20 minutes. The water should cover screw-tops or reach corks, which must be tied down with string, strong cloth or wire.

After sterilizing, tighten screw-tops and press in corks firmly. If using corks, leave to cool and dry, then dip the

neck of the bottle into melted paraffin wax (see page 47) to cover the corks and 1 cm ($\frac{1}{2}$ inch) down the neck of the bottle.

Cold method: Add I Campden Tablet dissolved in 1 tablespoon warm water to each 600 ml (1 pint) liquid. These tablets are usually available in shops selling wine-making equipment or chemists. They may cause the colour to fade a little but do not affect the flavour.

FRUIT LIQUEURS

These are made by steeping fruit, sometimes with other ingredients, in spirits until they flavour the liquid, with sugar added to sweeten. The best spirits to use are brandy vodka, gin, whisky or white rum. If the flavour of the fruit improves with stewing, the fruit is cooked in wine rather than water and sugar added at that stage.

Infusing: Leave the bottle or jar in a warm place, preferably in a sunny window, stirring occasionally, until the desired flavour is achieved and the sugar has dissolved. Strain and pour into sterilized bottles (see page 5). Seal with sterilized corks (see left).

Illustrated below: Serving suggestions for syrups. Ice cream with blackcurrant syrup; Fruit salad with orange syrup; Strawberry milkshake and Strawberry soda (made from strawberry syrup)

Orange Syrup

600 ml (1 pint) fresh
   orange juice (from
   about 8 large
   oranges)
1 kg (2 lb) sugar
juice of 1 lemon

Mix all the ingredients together in a pan. Heat gently, stirring, until the sugar has dissolved, then bring to the boil. Pour into hot sterilized bottles and sterilize.

Makes about 1.2 litres (2 pints)

NOTE: Lemon syrup can be made in the same way.

Blackcurrant Syrup

1 kg (2 lb) black-
   currants
600 ml (1 pint) cold
   water
sugar (see below)

Put the blackcurrants in a basin and crush with a potato masher. Stir in the water. Cover completely with a board and a tea-towel and leave until bubbles of gas form on the surface, showing the fruit has begun to ferment.

Mash again, then strain through a jelly bag, squeezing to extract as much juice as possible. Measure the juice and add 500 g (1 lb) sugar to each 600 ml (1 pint). Stir until the sugar is dissolved. Pour into hot sterilized bottles and sterilize.

Makes about 900 ml (1½ pints)

Strawberry Syrup

1 kg (2 lb) ripe
   strawberries
sugar (see below)

Cut the strawberries into small pieces, put in a basin and crush with a potato masher. Stand the basin in a pan of simmering water and leave until the juice runs very freely. Crush again.

Strain through a jelly bag, squeezing out as much juice as possible. Measure the juice and add 500 g (1 lb) sugar to each 600 ml (1 pint). Stir until the sugar is dissolved. Pour into hot sterilized bottles and sterilize.

Makes about 900 ml (1½ pints)

NOTE: Strawberry syrup can also be made in the same way as Blackcurrant syrup; strawberries usually ferment in 1 to 2 days.

Mint Syrup

There are several varieties of mint, e.g. ginger mint, pineapple mint, and they all make delicious syrup.

40–50 g (1½–2 oz)
  fresh mint leaves,
  without stalks
500 g (1 lb) sugar
600 ml (1 pint)
  cold water

Tear the mint leaves into pieces and place in a basin with the sugar. Mix well, crushing the mint and sugar together to extract the flavour of the mint. Stir in the water to dissolve the sugar.

Pour into a pan, bring to the boil and simmer for 15 minutes. Cover and leave for 24 hours.

Bring slowly to the boil, simmer for 5 minutes then strain through a jelly bag. Squeeze the leaves to extract as much juice as possible. Bring back to the boil, then pour into hot sterilized bottles and sterilize.

Makes about 750 ml (1¼ pints)

Lemon Squash

8 large lemons
450 ml (¾ pint) cold
   water
sugar (see below)
15 g (½ oz) citric acid

Pare the rind from 4 of the lemons. Peel all the lemons, discarding the white pith. Cut up the flesh, removing pips.

Put the rind and fruit pulp in an electric blender with the water and work until very smooth; strain if liked. Measure the juice and add 500 g (1 lb) sugar to each 600 ml (1 pint). Stir until the sugar is dissolved, then add the citric acid. Pour into hot, sterilized bottles and sterilize.

Makes about 1.75 litres (3 pints)

NOTE: Orange squash can be made in the same way, using 4 large oranges.

Ginger Beer

GINGER BEER PLANT:
6 sultanas
juice of 1 lemon
2 teaspoons sugar
1 teaspoon ground
  ginger
½ teaspoon lemon
  pulp
150 ml (¼ pint)
  cold water

Put all the ingredients in a screw-topped jar and leave for 3 days. On each of the next 4 days add 1 teaspoon sugar and ½ teaspoon ground ginger. On the following day, strain and add the juice of 1 lemon to the liquid.

GINGER BEER:
250 g (8 oz) sugar
300 ml (½ pint)
  boiling water
1.5 litres (2½ pints)
  cold water

Dissolve the sugar in the boiling water, then add the cold water. Pour onto the strained ginger beer plant. Mix and pour into sterilized screw-topped bottles or jars. It will be ready to drink after about 3 weeks.
Makes about 1.6 litres (2¾ pints)
NOTE: If a continuous supply is wanted, double the ingredients for the plant and also double the daily feed. After straining, retain half the sediment, add 150 ml (¼ pint) cold water and continue to feed as above.

Apricot Liqueur

1 kg (2 lb) apricots,
  stoned
600 ml (1 pint)
  white wine
250 g (8 oz) sugar
1 teaspoon allspice
  berries
600 ml (1 pint)
  brandy

Put the apricots and wine in an
enamelled pan and bring to the boil.
Simmer until the apricots are soft,
then mash.

Add the sugar and allspice berries
and stir until the sugar has dissolved.
Pour into a bottle or jar, cover and
leave in a warm place for 4 to 5 days.

Strain, squeezing out all the juice.
Add the brandy, pour into sterilized
bottles and cork tightly.

Makes about 1.75 litres (3 pints)

NOTE: To improve the flavour, crack
the apricot stones, blanch and skin the
kernels and add to the liquid as it
infuses. Alternatively, the stones may
be used to make Apricot stone liqueur
as for Cherry stone liqueur (see below).

Cherry Stone Liqueur

stones from 500 g
  (1 lb) cherries
600 ml (1 pint)
  brandy
250 g (8 oz) sugar

Wash and thoroughly dry the cherry
stones. Crush them with a heavy
rolling pin and put in a jar with the
brandy. Add the sugar, cover and
shake well. Leave in a warm place for
about 1 month. Strain, pour into
sterilized bottles and cork tightly.

Makes about 900 ml (1$\frac{1}{2}$ pints)

NOTE: Other fruit stones, one type only
or a mixture, can be made into liqueurs.

Coffee Bean Liqueur

9 Mocha coffee beans
600 ml (1 pint)
  white rum
250 g (8 oz) sugar

Put the coffee beans in a bottle or jar
and pour in the rum. Cover and leave
in a warm place for about 2 months.

Add the sugar, shake well and leave
until dissolved. Strain, pour into
sterilized bottles and cork tightly.

Makes about 900 ml (1$\frac{1}{2}$ pints)

Blackcurrant Liqueur (Cassis)

500 g (1 lb)
   blackcurrants,
   topped and tailed
1 × 3.5 cm (1½ inch)
   stick cinnamon
2 or 3 cloves
6 fresh blackcurrants
   leaves (optional)
600 ml (1 pint)
   brandy
350 g (12 oz) sugar

Put the blackcurrants in a basin and mash with a potato masher. Put in a bottle with the spices and leaves, if using. Add the brandy and sugar, cover tightly and leave in a warm place for 1 to 2 months.

   Strain, squeezing out as much juice as possible, pour into sterilized bottles and cork tightly.

Makes about 900 ml (1½ pints)

Damson Liqueur

500 g (1 lb) damsons
500 g (1 lb) sugar
600 ml (1 pint) gin

Prick the damsons very well and put in a jar or bottle with the sugar. Cover tightly and leave to stand for 2 to 3 days or until the juice runs freely.

   Pour in the gin and cover tightly. Leave in a warm place for about 2 months.

   Strain, squeezing out as much juice as possible, pour into sterilized bottles and cork tightly.

Makes about 900 ml (1½ pints)

Orange Liqueur

36 sugar cubes
3 large oranges,
   Seville if possible
600 ml (1 pint)
   white rum

Rub the sugar cubes against the oranges until they are deep orange in colour, showing they have absorbed the essential oil from the rind.

   Remove the white pith from the oranges and cut up the flesh, discarding the pips. Put the sugar, orange flesh and rum in a jar or bottle, cover tightly and leave in a warm place for 3 to 5 days. Strain, pour into sterilized bottles and cork tightly.

Makes about 900 ml (1½ pints)

INDEX

Acknowledgments

Photography by Melvin Grey
Food prepared by Heather Lambert
Designed by Astrid Publishing Consultants Ltd